LAST DAYS GLORY

A Vision That Changed One Woman's Thinking About
The End Times in America

By

Deborah Williams

LAST DAYS GLORY
By
Deborah Williams

ISBN-13: 978-1974578221
ISBN-10: 1974578224

By Deborah Williams, Author

Publisher: FirestarterPublications.com
P.O. Box 961, Huntsville, Arkansas 72740

Editor: Amy Shomaker
Proofreader: Zoe Edward White

Scripture quotations herein are from the King James Version, copyright © 1976 by Thomas Nelson, Inc. Nashville, Tennessee.

To Julie, my good good friend.

Our walks, talks and prayers have taken us through some
rough times. I couldn't have made it without you dear
sister in Christ. I thank the LORD for you.
He knew we would be friends long before we did
and that in itself is amazing.

CONTENTS

8

CHAPTER 1

A GLORIOUS NIGHT VISION

In 1993 God gave me an extraordinary night vision. In it the time was late, about midnight. I was with a friend in a Volkswagen Beetle. It was like the one I used to have in 1970.

In reality, the friend was not anyone I knew at the time. We were headed east down a lonely stretch of country road. It was an ink-black night. No light was visible anywhere except the headlights of the car. The moon was not shining. Not even a star was visible. We had just been remarking on how dark the night seemed, when suddenly in the distant sky there appeared a golden glow about ten o'clock high.

As we watched, the brilliance of the light intensified more and more as it drew nearer and the clouds began to boil around and through the light as if a tempest was brewing in the heavens. It seemed very unusual because there was no sound, no lightning and no thunder. Suddenly, bursting through the center of those radiant turbulent clouds appeared a team of mighty horses and a chariot very much like the type we've all seen in the movies depicting the days of the Roman gladiators. This team came charging toward us at a full-out gallop faster than any horses I had ever seen on earth.

In the chariot there stood a man. He was firmly gripping the reins in his right hand, and instantly I knew this was the Lord Jesus Christ Himself. With great excitement I thought, "This must be the rapture!" The joy of the LORD filled our vehicle, as the light spread across the night sky from east to west. This unearthly holy light seemed to emanate from the chariot, the horses and the Man. Then in an instant the whole heavens were ablaze with the glory of it all. In breathless anticipation I turned to my companion and asked, "Do you see Him? Do you see Jesus?"

"Yes! Yes! I see Him!" she shouted in delight.

Expecting at any moment to be elevated out of the vehicle into the air I asked, "Do you feel light yet?" I was expecting at any moment for gravity to lose its grip on us.

"No, I don't," she cried, perplexed, dismayed. Neither did I. Nor could I understand the meaning of this great and awesome scene we were witnessing together. It became clear to me that we were both seeing the same vision, and we were both thinking it must be the rapture. Indeed, there was no doubt in my mind that if it was indeed the rapture I was not going to miss it.

As the chariot raced on toward us, I began to understand this was a vision. Jesus was revealing himself to us. Then as I gazed in awe and amazement I realized the radiant, billowing clouds could be seen clearly through the oncoming chariot, the horses and the Man. The figures were as if they were made of transparent glass, and had the appearance of liquid, molten gold. Looking at the scene was like gazing into the opening of a glass-blower's furnace but without the intense heat.

Now the Lord was directly in front of us, merely a few hundred yards away riding in the clouds and many times bigger than life. The chariot began a sweeping turn toward the North. I could see the face of Jesus plainly now. He was smiling a smile of perfect peace. It was a peace like I'd never before experienced in my life. His gaze seemed to seep into my very soul, and without words He said with His gaze, "Take courage my daughter. Everything is under my control. There is nothing to fear."

As the chariot began to turn northward, he reached out his left hand and beckoned to me in a sweeping gesture that very clearly gave me an instruction, or perhaps I should say, an invitation to follow. It said without doubt, "I want you to come with me," and within my heart there was absolutely no hesitation. By the time we arrived at the place where the chariot turned, the vision went up from us and disappeared as suddenly as it had appeared.

There we were still in the little old Volkswagen, very much earthbound and everything the same as it was. The dark night that was closing back in around us, seemed like a living breathing force that tried to overwhelm and convince us that what we had seen was merely the result of our over-active imaginations, as if Jesus and His fiery chariot and golden horses of glory had never appeared at all.

My friend began to weep sorrowfully, "Oh, why did He leave us here?" she cried.

But the peace I had witnessed on the face of Jesus had somehow seeped into my soul, and I comforted her by saying, "I don't understand, but I know it is okay. I know He hasn't left us." With these words she looked at me hopefully and with a tiny smile dried her eyes.

As my vision in the night continued, I kept driving down the road where we had turned northward to follow the chariot. In no time at all we came to the home of a believing friend. Even though it was late, the lights were ablaze throughout the house, throwing golden beams of radiance through the open blinds and spilling onto the lawn. I marveled that the light coming from the house was very like the glory of Jesus pouring across the sky.

We entered through the front door. There in the living room sat a dozen people or more. I did not know any of them in real life. All of them were crying. Some were wailing. One man was wringing his hands. So we asked them if they had seen the LORD to which they all replied that they had indeed. And also like my friend, they had immediately thought the rapture had taken place and they had been left behind.

Then I heard someone weeping bitterly in the kitchen, so I left my friend with the admonition to comfort those in the living room while I went to see what was happening. There I spoke with another woman. I tried to comfort her with the same words I had told my friend, but she was comfortless, assured that the rapture had come and she had been left.

At last I told her, "You know my mother, Clara Williams don't you?" She nodded that she did. "Well look, if there's anyone I know that is going in the rapture, it's her! Let me go and see what she thinks and I'll come back and let you know." I ran out the open back door and across the front yard, and was immediately at my mother's house.

Even at such a late hour all the lights were on as if to banish the darkness that wanted to take over the world around us and once again I noted the light was spilling out onto the lawn. My mother sat at her kitchen table, crying. As I entered I called, "Oh Mom! Did you see the LORD?"

"Yes, I saw Him," she cried. Tears of disappointment streamed down her sweet lovely face. "Why didn't He take us home? Why did he leave us here?" she continued. In the background I could hear a TV tuned into the Trinity

Broadcasting Network. While trying to comfort my mother I could hear the TBN Director, Paul Crouch attempting to explain that the studio was being bombarded with phone calls.

"We can't believe what, what, what is happening," he stammered. Obviously he was at a loss for words. "The station is being flooded with phone calls from Christians all over America. They're all saying the same thing. They're saying they have seen the LORD! Yes! You heard me right. People from across the Nation are calling us. Many wonderful Christians, some of whom we know personally. They're all saying they've had a vision of something like the coming of the Lord. Yes! This is unbelievable, but they're saying He was riding in a chariot on the clouds in a ball of fire! Folks, I'll be honest with you. I don't know what it means, but I want to encourage you. Don't be afraid. The LORD hasn't left us."

And immediately I woke up. It was January 7, 1993 – more than 24 years ago.

When I awoke it was still dark outside. Thinking on the vision I realized I felt absolutely no distress over it. I sat on the edge of my bed, praying and meditating, but I received no confirmation. That day I related the vision separately to my Mother and again to my Father. Both are ministers of the Gospel and they each felt it meant the LORD was going to reveal Himself to His people.

CHAPTER 2

SCRIPTURES ALWAYS CONFIRM

For many days I questioned God about the night vision. I knew if it was from Him, His Word would verify it. No dream or vision should be taken at face value. If it is from God the scriptures will be in agreement with it. If they do not agree then the dream or vision should be tossed out on the trash heap!

As a minister myself, I could think of nowhere in the Word that spoke of such an occurrence. If it was there God would simply have to reveal it to me. After many days of prayer and searching the Word, I finally set the vision "on the shelf" so to speak and left it there. Three weeks went by. Late one evening I was worshipping and communing with the Lord in prayer when the voice of the Holy Spirit spoke very clearly to my heart, "Read the last chapter of Isaiah." I thought perhaps He wanted to give me a message to preach, so I opened my Bible and began to read as if I had never read Isaiah 66 before. From the first verse I was captivated.

In Isaiah 66:1 God asks:

"Where is the place of my rest?"

I hope you are not absolutely shocked at what I am about to say, but here goes. At least one place that God apparently finds a place of rest is in the believer's born-again spirit! It went on to say that the Lord reveals Himself to the person with "a contrite spirit and to him that trembles at His Word." The more I read the more thrilling it became. Verse 5 says:

"Hear the Word of the Lord, ye that tremble at His Word; your brethren that hated you, that cast you out for my name's sake, said, Let the Lord be glorified; but He shall appear to your joy, and they shall be ashamed."

It seems to me that Isaiah is not just writing to Israel, but to all who believe and reverentially fear the Word of God. Isaiah's message went on to report of hearing "a voice from the temple, a voice of the Lord that rendereth recompense to his enemies." Wow! If we are His temple, then does it follow that he speaks through us to render recompense on His enemies? Something to think about...

Then came the promise that Zion (the Church) would travail and God would bring forth a nation in one day. In verse 10, God said to "rejoice with Jerusalem." In verse 12 He promises to "extend peace to her like a river." In verse 13 God also promises, "As one whom his mother comforteth, so will I comfort you."

This was really wonderful, but I had no idea the confirmation of the night vision was about to burst upon my senses. Then verse 15 leaped off the page:

> "For, behold, the Lord will come with fire, and with his chariots like a whirlwind, to render his anger with fury, and his rebuke with flames of fire."

The Words seemed to explode in my heart and mind! It was right there! The answer to all my questions. Here was a scripture I had never "seen" before – the Lord coming with fire and chariots in a stormy wind! Even though I had read Isaiah a dozen times, I had never before realized such a thing was in the Bible. I could hardly believe the Words I was reading on the page. I read them over and over. I felt like I was experiencing the Word in living color, like a dream unfolding as truth.

Now that I had my hands on a confirming scripture where the LORD indeed will come in a chariot and flames of fire, I wanted more. And it came to me in Nahum 1:3:

> "The Lord is slow to anger, and great in power, and will not at all acquit the wicked: the Lord hath his way in the whirlwind and in the storm, and the clouds are the dust of his feet."

I recalled the vision to mind. Yes indeed, a storm was brewing and the clouds like dust were under the wheels of His chariot.

The scriptures began to open to me more and more on the subject. I began to see revelation everywhere. In 2 Kings chapter 6, we have the story of the Syrian army coming to find Elisha to take him captive. Elisha's servant went out early one morning and discovered they were surrounded by chariots and horsemen. Terrified he ran to Elisha in verse 15 and asked in fright, "What shall we do?" And how did Elisha respond? Look at verse 16:

> "Fear not, for they that be with us are more than they that be with them."

What a comfort to our hearts in times of trouble. Then in verse 17 of the same story, Elisha prays:

> "Lord, I pray thee, open his eyes, that he may see. And the Lord opened the eyes of the young man; and he saw: and behold, the mountain was full of horses and chariots of fire round about Elisha."

The opening of the eyes always signifies revelation. This only further confirmed Isaiah 66:3 where he said He reveals Himself to those who have a contrite spirit. Certainly, in my vision of the night the eyes of God's people in America were opened to see Jesus in a chariot of fire. The enlightenment which comforted Elisha's servant came as a result of prayer. He had compassion on his servant, because he was afraid.

The following scriptures also seemed to relate to it in Daniel 7:13:

> "I saw in the night visions, and, behold, one like the Son of man came with the clouds of heaven, and came to the Ancient of days, and they brought him near before him."

Now that my eyes were open I seemed to see the Lord in the clouds of heaven everywhere! Once again, the Lord is revealed in a fiery chariot in Psalm 68:17:

> "The chariots of God are twenty thousand, even thousands of angels: the Lord is among them, as in Sinai, in the holy place."

This reference to Sinai is the place where God came down on Mount Sinai and to the Israelites below it appeared to be on fire. Also we are told that God has angels riding in 20,000 chariots and the LORD is with them! Hallelujah! What a powerful Word. Even Jesus himself said He would come in the clouds of heaven in Matthew 26:64:

> "Jesus saith unto him... Hereafter shall ye see the Son of man sitting on the right hand of power and coming in the clouds of heaven."

Look at the awesome story of Elijah's ascent into heaven in 2 Kings 2:11-12. It says:

> "And it came to pass, as they still went on, and talked, that behold, there appeared a chariot of fire and horses of fire, and parted them both asunder; and Elijah went up by a whirlwind into heaven. And Elisha saw it, and he cried, My

father, my father, the chariot of Israel, and the horsemen thereof."

Never before had I realized that if Elisha had not seen it not only would he not have received a double portion of the ministry of Elijah, but we would have no witness of a chariot of fire taking Elijah up in a whirlwind to heaven. No doubt this was important for God's servants to know about. It seems to me if a chariot of fire took Elijah up to heaven, certainly our LORD can also appear in a chariot of fire coming down from heaven.

CHAPTER 3

NOW IS THE TIME

Immediately after receiving the scriptures cited above I was diligent to type it into a file on my computer. I also printed it out and carried it around with me for a long time. Due to a computer crash, all I had left other than my memory was my one printed copy. Since I had no leading of the Holy Spirit to share it publicly, I eventually laid the night vision aside in pursuit of other things.

Near the end of 2012 I began to have a yearning to revisit it. For months I searched for the papers on which they were printed. Finally I gave up looking and prayed, "LORD if you gave me this night vision you will have to restore it to me somehow in your timing."

One morning in March of 2013 I was worshipping the LORD and opened an old song book. There it was – the one and only dog-eared copy of the original printing of my vision. It felt like I had been handed a precious gift. I devoured every word like a person half-starved. I cried. I laughed. I rejoiced. It all came rushing back to me. It was as real as if I had just experienced it the night before.

Still a bit of sadness settled down on me. I was no closer to understanding the vision then, than I had been in 1993. I sought God earnestly for a time but it seemed like I had hit a high rock wall with a door that was dead-bolted tight. Neither did I have a key with which to open it. After a time I guess I just gave up and quit trying to figure it out. It frustrated me, so once again I laid the papers aside. This time I put the hard-copy where I knew I would find them again – nestled among the other dreams, visions and prophecies God had given me through the years. Perhaps,

I should have fasted and prayed like Daniel but it did not occur to me.

Three years went by. Now it was sometime in 2016, and I began to share the night vision with my prayer partner and best friend Julie. I said, "Wait a minute." And I ran to get the folder from my files. As I began to read it to her, it all came back to me and as it did, I had a great shock. I realized I was telling the night vision to the lady who had been with me in the Volkswagen. Julie was my friend in the vision. And now she was my best friend in real life. I did not meet her until the Autumn of 2013 when she and her family walked into the Church meeting where I attended. Suddenly I realized why I could not understand the vision, because it was not yet time for God to reveal it or for me to share it!

From that moment of revelation to this moment of writing a fire has burned in my heart with the promise that Jesus is going to soon reveal Himself to His people in our Nation. It will be a revelation like there has never been in the history of the Faith. There has never been a witness of thousands of believers all seeing the same vision. I believe it is going to burst upon the American believers all at once. They are going to know Jesus in a way they have never imagined. They are going to see Him corporately! In the vision, the LORD will bring home these truths to us:

1. There is no need to fear because He is in control.

2. Everything that is about to happen is according to God's perfect plan and in His perfect time.

3. He is going to go forth to conquer His enemies which are our enemies.

4. We are going to rise up and follow Him as the LORD leads us into spiritual battle.

Not long after reading the night vision to my friend Julie, I knew I needed detailed understanding. First, I rewrote it into a new document on my computer. Much of what you have read was quite scattered, but I finally had it on the computer. I just "knew" as I rewrote it the understanding would come.

It didn't.

It was obvious to me that the time was swiftly approaching for the fulfillment of the vision, if for no other reason than I now knew my friend in the night vision. Another reason is the spiritual, political and economic climate in which we now live. More importantly was the understanding that God wanted to both warn and comfort His people in America for what is drawing closer. Last of all was this scripture. He gave it to me in the early days of my ministry and in recent times it has come alive to me. These Words were given to Ezekiel. They have strengthened me to wait before God. It begins in chapter 12, verse 26:

> "Again the word of the LORD came to me, saying. Son of man, behold, they of the house of Israel say, The vision that he seeth is for many days to come, and he prophesieth of the times that are far off. Therefore say unto them, Thus saith the Lord GOD; There shall none of my words be prolonged any more, but the word which I have spoken shall be done, saith the Lord GOD."

A short time later as I was worshipping the Lord in the Spirit, the meaning of the night vision began to unfurl like sheets waving on a clothesline. The wind of the Spirit was blowing again. I began to meditate upon the thoughts that seemed to be downloading into my mind. I sat down to begin to write and was interrupted by an urgent phone call. One emergency after another began to assault me. After three days, life calmed down and I went to sit at the computer fully expecting the revelation to all come galloping back to me.

I reread what I had written, but no matter how much I worshipped, prayed, repented, sang and sat quietly meditating nothing came. Absolutely nothing. I tried for days to get to that place but to no avail. The way back seemed to be cut off as if the bridge was out. This is another scripture that I have held onto for many years, found in Habakkuk 2:2-3:

> "And the LORD answered me, and said, Write the vision, and make it plain upon tables, that he may run that readeth it. For the vision is yet for an appointed time, but at the end it shall speak, and not lie: though it tarry, wait for it; because it will surely come, it will not tarry."

I am writing this for you, dear Reader. If these bear witness with your spirit, then run with the visions I tell you because I have no doubt they are from the LORD. He will bring them to pass. At the end the vision will speak.

Here it is July 2017 and once again the LORD has called me to write and has given me the order to let nothing stop me. In fact, a prophet of God from Malawi just recently gave me a Word, saying, "Nothing shall ever stop you again. You shall walk over every enemy and remove every hindrance. From this day you shall be unstoppable!"

I believe it! So now I am acting on the Word of God's Prophets, both then and now. I must declare what I have seen. Isaiah 21:6 says:

"For thus hath the LORD said unto me, Go, set a watchman, let him declare what he seeth."

And so I have some declarations to declare based upon the night vision and the scriptures the LORD has given me. Please let them stir your heart as they have mine. Read prayerfully with an open mind, because you may see things you've never seen before. Take them to the LORD and ask Him for confirmation. Do not let them disturb you, even if they upset some of your end times belief system. If they do and they are from the LORD He will show you the truth.

CHAPTER 4

DECLARATION NUMBER ONE

Dark times are coming to America, but God's glory will shine to us and through us like never before!

Understand me. I do not desire dark times. I do not ask God for them. I've been asked, "Can we hold these dark times back through prayer?" Yes, I believe we can, but will we? What kind of praying will that take? How dedicated are we to the call of the LORD? How earnest are we in our prayers for the lost? How many prayer warriors will it take? I don't know the answer to these questions. I do know that Jonah was sent to Nineveh and they repented at his preaching. Jesus even made mention of the Ninevites with approval, but it did not stop the destruction. It only delayed it. However, the subsequent delay was for more than 100 years! It did not come in the generation that heeded the preaching of Jonah.

I do know this, however. A time is coming soon where God is going to clearly make a separation between those who love Him and those who do not. This will come either with dark times or not. Remember the children of Israel down in the land of Egypt? The first plague that came upon the Egyptians that did not come upon the Israelites was darkness. It was said of that darkness that it could be felt. Look at these verses in Exodus 10:21-23:

> "And the LORD said unto Moses, Stretch out thine hand toward heaven, that there may be darkness over the land of Egypt, even darkness which may be felt. And Moses stretched forth his hand toward heaven; and there was a thick darkness in all the land of Egypt three days: They saw not one another, neither rose any from his place for three

days: but all the children of Israel had light in their dwellings."

The coming darkness is probably no great revelation to anyone by now, but I believe the shaking that is coming is far worse than anything we have imagined. In the night vision the darkness had a profound black quality about it. We could feel it. There were no stars, no moon, and no lights throughout all the countryside where we were traveling. The only light we had was coming from the little old vehicle I was driving. Clearly the only spiritual light in those days will be coming from those of us who love the LORD. We see this stated plainly in the Word of God in 2 Corinthians 4:6 yet we often overlook it because it does not seem real to us:

> "For God, who commanded the light to shine out of darkness, hath shined in our hearts, to give the light of the knowledge of the glory of God in the face of Jesus Christ."

The light of the glory of God is on the face of Jesus and His light is in us because we know Him! God wants us to show forth that light to people who are lost in the darkness of this world system. Believers should not fear anything that is coming upon the world. Trust in the LORD. When difficult days come, believe that He will take you through and He will do great things for you.

It was also very late – almost midnight. I think we can all agree that it is very late on God's time clock. The later it gets on the prophetic timepiece, the darker it's going to get in this world – not just in America. In the Word of God darkness always refers to evil, and in the night vision it seemed like a living, breathing force that wanted to consume us.

25

The darkness of this world is led by the Prince of Darkness, who is the devil which is Satan. Every thought, word and action that denies giving JESUS CHRIST the absolute rule and lordship over our individual lives and the church corporately originates with the devil. But praise God for Colossians 1:13 that says:

> "Who hath delivered us from the power of darkness."

Jesus is about to reveal Himself as the absolute LORD to His church, but before He does so it may appear the enemy has won the battle. The Father is sending many warnings to us, saying get ready for what is about to happen. The coming darkness is going to be intense, as if it is trying to devour us. This will only serve to drive the true church in this Nation closer together than ever before.

It is noteworthy that I understood from the night vision that the body of Christ in America would be meeting in houses. At the time that was a rare occurrence, but now it is commonplace. In the dark times that are approaching it will become imperative. Many great church edifices will be filled with apostates, while many small ones will be empty, shut down, and locked for lack of funding to keep the doors open.

Even now I am not sure if the darkness which is coming is spiritual or literal or both. I will not make a pronouncement on that score. Whichever way it comes to us, God's people are going to shine in the midst of the darkness. I love the verses in Isaiah 60:1-3 that say:

> "Arise, shine; for thy light is come, and the glory of the LORD is risen upon thee. For, behold, the darkness shall cover the earth, and gross darkness

26

the people: but the LORD shall arise upon thee, and his glory shall be seen upon thee. And the Gentiles shall come to thy light, and kings to the brightness of thy rising."

Please understand this is not meant to be a message of gloom and doom. The LORD has not told me exactly what the coming storm is, but I know I will recognize it when I see it. And when it comes He is going to reveal Himself to His people. As the darkness get darker, His revelation will come nearer to us, and the light is going to get brighter and brighter for the believer. Proverbs 4:18 gives us this promise:

"But the path of the just is as the shining light, that shineth more and more unto the perfect day."

CHAPTER 5

DECLARATION NUMBER TWO

When God's glory shows up the fruit of real repentance and humility will be apparent in His people.

Did you notice we were in an old Volkswagen Beetle? The meaning of this may be literal. Perhaps only old vehicles will be running due to the detonation of an EMP (electromagnetic pulse) in the atmosphere above this country. Or perhaps we will no longer be able to afford to fix the multitude of things that can go wrong with our computer driven vehicles of today. Or the meaning of this may be merely spiritual. Whatever the case, I know one thing for sure. Those little vehicles speak clearly of humility, meekness and lowliness of heart, which will be notable qualities in the body of believers in the coming last-days.

In January 1984 God called me to a thirty day fast, which is a type of humbling yourself. I didn't know it at the time but it was a necessary preparation for the ministry into which God was about to propel me. I had already obeyed God to quit my well-paying job and go to a Summer Boot Camp for Ministers. I did not know that God was about to open doors to launch the Prophetic call on my life. Surely there is nothing better than fasting to enable you to begin to clearly hear the Voice of the LORD.

On the seventeenth day of my fast I awakened abruptly to a storm that burst upon my apartment. Horrific lightning flashed and thunder roared in a deafening crescendo. I opened my eyes and saw to my astonishment that the storm was not outside, but inside my room. I literally fell out of the bed onto the floor. The instant I touched the carpet, the storm ceased and the Voice of the Holy Spirit began to speak to me. The words poured into my mind until I cried, "LORD, please wait. Please let me get a pen and paper," and the words stopped like turning off a faucet. I reached for something to write with and the words started again. This is what I wrote:

"What do you hear?" the Voice asked. I replied, "I hear the thunder." The Voice continued, "You hear a new sound, a noise like you have never heard before. You hear the sound of coming judgment. You hear the Voice of the One who spoke out of Mount Sinai unto the people of God. This voice caused them to tremble with great fear because of their sinfulness before God. Instantly they understood their minuteness before a great and mighty God. To them the Voice was terrifying, so they told Moses they did not want to hear it again. All those who did not believe died in the wilderness. I have enabled you to hear the Voice as thunder so you will understand it as a warning of an approaching storm that is going to burst upon this Nation. When it comes only those who are hiding in the Secret Place of the Most High will have no fear. They will feel no alarm. To them the Storm will be an assurance of real peace and provision by My Hand. Only those in the Secret Place will be safe from harm. A great storm is indeed coming. You will see it. Just as you have seen and heard it here in this room. And just as it came suddenly without warning so will it come to America. Torrential rains and dreadful lightning will flow out over the land. It will be so astonishing that every nation and every tongue will tremble at what they hear and see and they will hide for the fear of judgment coming to their land as well. Fear not, for those who hide in the Cleft of the Rock shall stand and not fall. They will see the storm pass by and not be afraid. They will know their God and give witness to His power and might. The effects of this storm will shine into many hearts and multitudes will repent of their idolatries against me. As the storm passes over I will hide you with my hand as I hid the Israelites from the death angel and no harm came to their firstborn children. Neither shall it harm you. My blood covenant stands with you forever. No harm will come to those who will humble themselves, will wash their hands clean and have pure hearts. These will see the salvation of God, for He is merciful and kind and will demonstrate toward them diverse blessings too numerous to number. They will see miraculous provision as no generation of my servants has ever seen. Now are the days to wash your garments from the filthiness of the flesh. Those that refuse and think they will be able to stand before me in uncleanness without true holiness shall be left out of the Camp. They shall be caught unawares. The storm shall burst upon them suddenly and they will cry out for deliverance, but I will not hear. They will call but I will not answer. Understand it is not because I do not care for them that I do not answer their cry, but when the storm hits it will be too late to prepare. So take heed to yourself. Do not judge others, but judge yourself. Do not compare yourself to anyone but your God, for even though this day may be long in coming it is coming as surely as My Son. Beware, lest you who have been warned of the approaching storm, fall and be left out of the camp and therefore are ravaged with the enemies of God like a beast of the field without shelter.

Only once have I spoken this Word to a group of believers. When I finished reading, I looked up and the entire assembly was prostrate on the floor crying and repenting before the LORD. (I might add that the Ninevites did exactly the same thing in the book of Jonah.) It is a hard word but by now we have heard many such warnings. The time is very near. The urgency for me to get this message into print is strong. He has even ordered me not to go back to work until it is finished. I do not want to stand before God and have to give an answer for those who would have read my simple words and finally "got it" but didn't, because I didn't write it. I believe many wishy-washy, spineless believers who have not been able to make a stand for righteousness will finally do so simply because of my obedience.

The LORD is near to you even at this moment – waiting. Like myself, I see you reading these words and crying. That is a good thing. All you need to do is humble yourself before Him. Repent. Wait upon Him.

Repentance and waiting before God is an act of humility. By it you are saying, "I cannot do this on my own. He is my Father. I am His child. I need His help and direction." By humbling yourself in this way you will become a great light in the coming darkness. In Matthew 18:1-4 when his disciples came to him and asked who was the greatest in the kingdom of heaven Jesus answered in this way:

> "And Jesus called a little child unto him, and set him in the midst of them, And said, Verily I say unto you, Except ye be converted, and become as little children, ye shall not enter into the kingdom

of heaven. Whosoever therefore shall humble himself as this little child, the same is greatest in the kingdom of heaven."

Waiting before God is simple. If you do not know how, then here is a suggestion that works for me. Just shut off everything around you that is vying for your attention. It might be your phone, your entertainment, your family, or your job. Just as a waiter comes to your table and takes your order and brings out your food, talk to God.

Let nothing sidetrack you. Wait with determination. Wait in expectancy with your Bible open. Wait with thankfulness in your heart. Sing songs of worship to Him. It may only take a few minutes. Or it may take hours. Or you may have to come before Him many times over the course of days, weeks or months. I think it depends on how serious you are and how great the demonic interference has been in your life. But if you are faithful, He will speak to your heart and reveal His will to you. Trust Him in childlike faith to show you what He wants you to do in order to prepare for the darkness that is coming. I'm not referring to stocking up food in your pantry although that is not a bad thing. I'm talking about being done with the lust of the world, the lust of the eyes and the pride of life (see I John 2:15-16), for those things witness against you that the love of God is not in you.

In the night vision all the saints were weeping. They had seen the glory of God. Many were sure they had missed the rapture because of some secret sin. Aren't we all in that position? Some may accuse me by saying, "In the vision you were not weeping." I think that is because God needed to show us there will be many saints in America that will be ready. They will understand the revelation. They will trust and not be afraid. I was merely a

32

representative of those saints. At any rate I have done my share of weeping and repentance since that time.

Look at Isaiah when he saw the glory of God in the temple. Isaiah 6:5 states:

> "Then said I, Woe is me! for I am undone; because I am a man of unclean lips, and I dwell in the midst of a people of unclean lips: for mine eyes have seen the King, the LORD of hosts."

This will be the genuine response of many when the glory of the LORD comes to the believers in this country, but thank God for the next two verses in Isaiah 6:6-7:

> "Then flew one of the seraphims unto me, having a live coal in his hand, which he had taken with the tongs from off the altar: And he laid it upon my mouth, and said, Lo, this hath touched thy lips; and thine iniquity is taken away, and thy sin purged."

I want to be one of the first who say in deep contrition, "Oh LORD, woe is me for I have impure lips. I live among tainted people. Forgive me. Forgive them. We speak things we should not speak and we don't speak things that we should!" Praise God we have His promise to cleanse us from every sin if we simply humble ourselves.

CHAPTER 6

DECLARATION NUMBER THREE

When darkness descends the believers in America will be as one in unity, forgiveness and love.

It is important to observe that I was not alone in the night vision. I was with a friend. Loneliness in the body of Christ is rampant. I believe it is a dreadful scourge from the enemy. Without reservation I want to announce:

LONELINESS IS COMING TO AN END IN THE BODY OF CHRIST!

I believe that God is once again going to send us out two by two just as in the days of His earthly pilgrimage. He did not intend for us to be alienated from each other. It is my firm belief that we are going to be one, and we will know each other by the Spirit of the LORD. We will suffer with those who are suffering and rejoice with those who are rejoicing. We are going to pray for our brothers and sisters in Christ and see them made whole – spiritually, emotionally, mentally and physically. Judgment of one another will end. In fact, I believe it has already begun. As the time approaches we will see gentleness and forgiveness break forth. It will be open and unashamed. We will become quick to receive reproof. Then God's miraculous provision will be seen in our midst. Many will be used of God to make provision for those in need.

We will take heed to words of wisdom, strength and encouragement from the rest of the body no matter how humble their place is in the body. All of us will be needed – even the little toes - members who do not seem to have it all together or be of any value. The "big shots" will cease to be giants in the Kingdom of God, for God is going to lift up the nobodies and they will illustrate mountain

34

moving faith to the body of Christ. Their faith will become contagious! And those who were once known as "big-shots" will become servants to all in the Name of the LORD.

Today many are running about saying, "I am a great Apostle." "I am a great Prophet." "I am this, or that or the other." God is going to reveal His true apostles and prophets and they will be humble servants, not seeking notoriety, not demanding submission and not ministering for hire! When darkness comes and the failing economy strips those who seek after compensation, they will be exposed at best as shams and at worst as charlatans. They will have no light in them, although they may masquerade as great and saintly persons. Don't be deceived, for even the devil himself parades about as an angel of light (2 Corinthians 11:14.) God's men and women who are about to rise on the scene will care only for loving the church, meeting its needs and seeing souls saved. Devoted service will be their motivation. By their devotion you will know them and the LORD will take care of their financial needs. They will be willing to minister wherever God sends them, whether it's behind the scenes or on a platform.

A new day of submission is coming into the hearts of genuine believers. Even the connotation of the word will change. It will not be a submission of sheep to shepherds. Nor will it be a lording over the flock by a controlling few, but a mutual submission amidst the sheep. Deference to one another is coming into the church. High esteem and honoring of all others will be a clear indicator of a person that is part of the true church in the coming season. No one will be putting himself or herself forward. Self-aggrandizement will cease. It will no longer be about self or my ministry but that of others.

We are going to discern the body of Christ. No one will have to tell you who they are and what they stand for. No one will care what ordination credentials you hold or if you have a 501(c)(3). It will become clear by the fruit of the Holy Spirit who is and who is not walking with God. And when this happens great healing and deliverance will come into the body of Christ in ways we have never even imagined. Healing is one of the main purposes of the communion service. Look at First Corinthians 11:26-33.

> "For as often as ye eat this bread, and drink this cup, ye do shew the Lord's death till he come. Wherefore whosoever shall eat this bread, and drink this cup of the Lord, unworthily, shall be guilty of the body and blood of the Lord. But let a man examine himself, and so let him eat of that bread, and drink of that cup. For he that eateth and drinketh unworthily, eateth and drinketh damnation to himself, not discerning the Lord's body. For this cause many are weak and sickly among you, and many sleep. For if we would judge ourselves, we should not be judged. But when we are judged, we are chastened of the Lord, that we should not be condemned with the world.Wherefore, my brethren, when ye come together to eat, tarry one for another."

We will be patient and tenderhearted toward one another. We will have genuine communion as the LORD's body, and through that communion we will be healed! Our English word for "communion" comes from the Greek word Koinonia. It also means "fellowship." First Corinthians 10:16 tells us that the cup of the LORD is our communion or our fellowship with the blood of Christ and the bread is our communion with the body of Christ. Verse 17 says:

> "For we being many are one bread and one body: for we are all partakers of that one bread."

Partaking of communion without dying to the self life is dangerous. This is what it means to partake unworthily. We risk drinking death to ourselves when we take communion with the body of Christ and harbor criticisms, offences or grievances in our hearts against someone else in the body. In so doing we are not discerning that we are part of one another. It is like cursing your hand or your foot and telling it to die. When we come to the table of the LORD in this way, we are defiling His body. The reason Jesus gave us "communion" was to remind us that we are one with Him. We are one in His suffering, one in His death and one in His resurrection power. Praise God! Should we have grievances against Him? No. Neither should we have any criticisms against each other. We are all part of Him. That is why He said in Matthew 5:23 & 24:

> "Therefore if thou bring thy gift to the altar, and there rememberest that thy brother hath ought against thee; Leave there thy gift before the altar, and go thy way; first be reconciled to thy brother, and then come and offer thy gift."

Right now the body is very disjointed because we are not being reconciled to one another. When you visit a new group where other believers are gathered, most of them have the "spirit of suspicion" rather than the "discerning of spirits." Furthermore, they are often so filled with their own judgments against one another they cannot discern what spirit has just walked into the room. Often they accept deceivers with wide open arms, smiling and greeting them joyfully, because these con artists are charismatic or have money or say all the right words. Heaven help us.

Even now many are being deceived by demons which are drawing them astray into apostasy. This is an antichrist spirit which is recognized by a "know-it-all" attitude. The spirit of error takes hold of them and their sin of pride is demonstrated by an adamant refusal to listen to correction. This pride will bring destruction into their lives. Ironically the destruction of their health, or their families or their wealth might be their only means of salvation. When they fall into a deep pit a few of them will actually receive help from the very ones they have misjudged and criticized. I pray this is not the case with any of whom I know and fellowship.

There seems to be many believers today being seduced by spirits that imitate the Holy Spirit through false teachers who offer a "sensuous, feel good" Christianity. Flocking after signs, wonders and miracles, they are led by teachers who only talk about love and grace, devoid of any soul-searching truth. There is no mention of holiness, heart purity and dying to the self-life. Often the deceived person has had hands laid upon them by false teachers and have received a demon by transference. These poor deluded souls appear to be more severely entrenched in sin than most. Since they have mistaken a demon spirit for the Holy Spirit and therefore believe they are hearing the LORD, it is difficult to get them delivered from bondage. They are listening to demons that give them all types of physical thrills and sensations that in some ways seem to mimic the Holy Ghost anointing. Often you will discover various hidden sexual sins in their lives such as extra-marital affairs, fornication, pornography with masturbation and homosexual encounters. If these are in your life but you think you are in love with Jesus think again. I am warning you now, the spirit you have is not the Holy Ghost! I plead with you to get help now. Find a fellow believer that is not afraid to pray for your deliverance, a person to whom you can be honest and not be judged. Find someone who will be patient with you and tell you the truth. It will take time for you to recognize the voice of the Holy Spirit again. If you cannot find someone, then get serious with God alone. Repent and turn away from the issues that plague you. Avoid those who drag you back. Fast. Pray. Saturate yourself in the Word of God and believe that He will lead you to someone who will rally around you and strengthen you. He is faithful. He will do it.

Today there are those who call themselves prophets or prophetesses but God did not send them. They move from place to place spewing out their so-called prophetic words in attempts to draw a following. They are critical of leaders, pastors or true prophets they cannot manipulate. They give false words of hope that tickle the ears of the hearers and these words do not come to pass, causing many to fall away. These are especially dangerous to the babes in Christ and the undiscerning.

Others are being held in bondage by religious Jezebel spirits and charismatic witchcraft spirits. They want to control how their church operates. They are talebearers and always are found in the middle of any trouble being stirred up in the group of believers where they attend.

Still others in the body of Christ are running from meeting to meeting trying to get more anointing. God cannot establish their hearts or get them rooted and grounded in a fellowship because they will not dedicate themselves to one. They see no need of being submitted to anyone and refuse deliverance. With deep sadness I know that some of those who reject deliverance and go on to pursue their self-willed, sensuous ways will become persecutors of the sanctified believers in the days ahead.

All of the above examples are just a few of the demonic infiltrations I am witnessing in the body of Christ. It is widespread and reveals the carnality holding sway in the church at this time. However, beloved friends, I know revival is coming. God is going to have a people that will repent of their stubborn strong-willed attitudes and vindictive words and submit to loving believers for reproof. This will bring great deliverance into the body of Christ. Even many who are in bondage to demonic spirits are going to be delivered and then God will use them to deliver others. Don't give up on these brothers and sisters. It may take a lot of patience, brokenness and love to help them, but some of them are coming out in Jesus' Name!

The unity that is approaching will not be a work of man, but the work of the Holy Spirit. America will see it and many will be saved as a result of the change they see in true believers. We are entering into the times for which Jesus himself prayed of the Father and His prayers will all be answered. John 17:21 speaks to what I am declaring:

> "That they all may be one; as thou, Father, art in me, and I in thee, that they also may be one in us: that the world may believe that thou hast sent me."

Did you catch that? The world will know that God sent Jesus to restore us back to the Father when they see the true church becoming one! That is our LORD's great desire. God's people in America will reveal it. We will not be left behind in anything God is doing in the earth!

CHAPTER 7

DECLARATION NUMBER FOUR

As American believers behold His glory we will walk in
supernatural peace, provision and power.

Before the coming of the LORD to establish His kingdom on earth and His thousand year reign, His glory will be revealed to and through His people all over the world. His glory is the witness that the Father loves His Son. Only by His glory can we be made one in heart, mind and purpose. This is stated clearly in the book of John in the prayer Jesus prayed for His disciples. Only then will the world see His glory. It must come through us! At the end of Declaration Number Three we saw the promise that the LORD will make us one in John 17:21. What is truly amazing is how it happens. Look at John 17:22-23:

> "And the glory which thou gavest me I have given them; that they may be one, even as we are one: I in them, and thou in me, that they may be made perfect in one; and that the world may know that thou hast sent me, and hast loved them, as thou hast loved me."

Did you see it? If not go back and reread it. Hidden within that verse is the revelation that the glory makes us one. Deborah's paraphrase goes like this: "Father, I'm giving those who believe in me the glory you gave me, so they can be one just like we are one." So, the glory is what makes us one with God and each other.

In the night vision the TBN director, Paul Crouch who is now in heaven was telling the Church in America not to be afraid. Thinking on it now, it seems to me he was acting as our communicator from heaven that all will be well with us. He was sharing the news with the entire listening audience that thousands of believers had seen the identical vision revealing the glory of the LORD and the vision they saw of the Him was even as He is. John the Revelator saw Him in the same manner – as the victorious, overcoming, glorious LORD of Hosts.

My mother is gone now too. Thinking about that takes me back to the night vision and my mother at the kitchen table crying. My mother was a great intercessor and her prayers are still being answered. Even though she is gone from me in the physical realm she is not far away. When we enter the glory, I know in my heart we will not be separated from those who are no longer with us on earth. When we behold the glory of God we will become one with the church in heaven.

So, as we get closer to our going home time, I declare the glory is coming to God's people in America. What was the fruit I received from seeing the LORD in the night vision? It was a supernatural peace given in a time of great distress. It came to me by simply beholding the LORD's glory. How much peace do you think Jesus has? That's how much peace He wants His people to have. I believe when we see His glory His supernatural peace will become ours.

Remember how God gave me Isaiah 66 as the confirmation to the night vision? In that chapter we see the English word "glory" five different times. In each instance it is translated from the Hebrew word "kabod" and refers to "weight, in a good sense." Figuratively it means "splendor or copiousness." Kabod comes from the root word "kabad" or "kabed." It is a primitive root also meaning "to be heavy or weighty, in a good sense (numerous, rich, honorable.)" *New Strong's Concise Dictionary of the Words in the Hebrew Bible," 1995*

Thomas Nelson Publishers, Inc. God promises in verse 12 of Isaiah 66:

> "Behold, I will extend peace to her like a river, and the glory of the Gentiles like a flowing stream:"

Notice that "glory" and "peace" are joined together. Notice as well that our provision is also assured. Several other translations state "the wealth of the nations" shall flow into it rather than using the word "glory." To who was this promise made? It was given to all those who tremble at God's Word which means they reverence and obey Him. So, the promise of God to extend peace like a river and give provision is not just to His people Israel but to all those who reverentially obey His Word. In the scripture Haggai 2:9 the Word says,

> "The glory of this latter house shall be greater than of the former, saith the LORD of hosts: and in this place will I give peace, saith the LORD of hosts."

So, we see that "glory" and "peace" are once again connected and they are very clearly credited to the latter house which at that time had a literal meaning. I believe it also refers to the church as being the latter spiritual house. The glory coming to this house will be as much greater in excellence as the glory of the Gospel surpasses the glory of the law. (See 2 Corinthians 3:10.) And in that house there will be great peace.

In the New Testament the word "glory" comes from the Greek word "doxa." This is an awesome little-big word. It is used to describe "the nature and acts of God in self-manifestation, i.e., what He essentially is and does." (Vine's Expository Dictionary of Old and New Testament

Words © 1981 by Fleming H. Revell Company.) In other words, God's glory is everything that God is and everything that God does! And Jesus wants us to have it! Wow! That is impossible to fathom.

Believers are about to see his glory. The church in America is about to become one with the church in heaven. Heaven is filled with God's glory. Stephen, the first martyr of the Church saw it in Acts 7:55:

> "But he, being full of the Holy Ghost, looked up steadfastly into heaven, and saw the glory of God, and Jesus standing on the right hand of God,"

Stephen was being stoned, yet even as they pummeled his body, he could only think to look up and when he did he saw the glory of God. He saw his beloved Savior Jesus Christ standing on the right hand of God. We know for a fact that Jesus is seated in heaven because the Word tells us. Mark says so in chapter 16, verse 19:

> "So then after the Lord had spoken unto them, he was received up into heaven, and sat on the right hand of God."

When the heavens opened, Jesus stood up. As Stephen was beholding Jesus, Jesus was beholding him! Don't you just imagine that all of the saints in heaven saw Jesus stand up and were looking at Stephen too? I think at that moment the supernatural peace that was on the face of Jesus in my night vision was on His face then when Stephen looked at him. And I believe that just as I experienced that peace so did Stephen. You may wonder why this is important. What does this have to do with us now? Everything. We are so often distressed in this life, but it is not the will of our Savior. All we need is to behold His glory and when we do His peace will flow out of Him and into us. He wants to fill us with His glory and his peace. Even more so when persecution arises against us. What a demonstration that will be to the unsaved that Jesus is alive and He loves them.

There are numerous depictions in the Word where the glory of God filled the house of the LORD. Today the house of the LORD is not a building but two or more individual believers or a corporate gathering of believers. We do not "go" to church. We "are" the church. In the temple built by Solomon it is said that the glory filled the temple and it was so heavy that the priests could not enter. This is what 2 Chronicles 7:1-2 says:

> "Now when Solomon had made an end of praying, the fire came down from heaven, and consumed the burnt offering and the sacrifices; and the glory of the LORD filled the house. And the priests could not enter into the house of the LORD, because the glory of the LORD had filled the LORD's house."

Why did the priests need to enter the temple? Because they were to offer the blood from the animal that was sacrificed on the altar. Now we have a high priest that offered his own blood as a sacrifice once and for all, who now is in heaven according to:

> Hebrews 4:14 "Seeing then that we have a great high priest, that is passed into the heavens, Jesus the Son of God, let us hold fast our profession."

> Hebrews 10:19-23 Having therefore, brethren, boldness to enter into the holiest by the blood of Jesus, By a new and living way, which he hath consecrated for us, through the veil, that is to say, his flesh; And having an high priest over the

45

house of God; Let us draw near with a true heart in full assurance of faith, having our hearts sprinkled from an evil conscience, and our bodies washed with pure water. Let us hold fast the profession of our faith without wavering; (for he is faithful that promised;)

We no longer need to offer the blood of animals, because Jesus by His own blood has made a way for us to come directly and boldly before the throne of God. (See Hebrews 4:16.) Now, we have been made spiritual priests and kings to offer sacrifices of praise to our God. When the glory comes upon the church, men will no longer be the ones doing the ministry. In this soon to be repentant, humble, honoring, submitting church only God will be the minister. When He uses us everyone will know it is God showing off not us!

A great deal of the visible church in America is more about their glory than His glory. Hence we have very little of God. That is going to change when the LORD reveals Himself to His people.

In the night vision, the brightness of his glory made us look up into heaven, even as Stephen. When we did, we saw the LORD for Who He is, and as we watched Him we knew what direction to take. All we had to do was follow him. As we followed in the direction He led us, we were immediately brought together with the body of Christ in that area.

As the LORD leads every member of His church we will see miracles like we have never dreamed. He will give us the provision we need to do His work. This last days church on earth is going to be the greatest demonstration of the power and authority of God that the world has ever seen.

CHAPTER 8

DECLARATION NUMBER FIVE

God's overcoming believers will gather a great harvest and prepare a people ready to meet the LORD.

Suddenly when the LORD reveals Himself, every true child of God in this Nation will KNOW Him, no matter how poor their spiritual condition may be right now. This revelation knowledge will bring great victory and genuine faith into the hearts of American believers. For the first time many will start thinking of others instead of themselves! Here are some examples of what I see coming:

- American believers will demonstrate supernatural peace in the storm.

- The joy of the LORD will enable us to endure hardness.

- The glory will make it possible for us to discern those who are not of Him.

- The doctrines of men will fall off of us.

- Weaklings will become spiritual giants overnight.

- We will be equipped to follow our Captain into battle.

- An overcoming church will arise and do healings & miracles to win the lost.

Furthermore, I believe this will happen before the Rapture. For too long much of the Church in America has had an escapism mentality. While much of the Church of Jesus is suffering unspeakable persecution all over the world, many American believers have little desire to occupy till He comes. Few are doing the business of the

Kingdom – the winning of souls to Christ. Many just want Jesus to get them out of here.

Don't take what I'm saying wrong and quit reading. Please hang on with me. However whether you do or don't, I must declare what I firmly believe:

Only the overcomers engaged in the Father's business will be ready for the rapture.

In my opinion the spirit of every Church mentioned in the book of Revelation is still with us. When the Apostle John had The Revelation of Jesus Christ certainly the churches of Asia were not the only Churches on earth. They were simply representative of the situations the LORD saw among His people.

Through the seven churches I believe the LORD was pointing out the temptations that had to be overcome in order to be ready to do His work and to meet Him in the rapture after the work is finished. As such, I believe the seven churches are signs and warnings to us of the problems and temptations in this present day that we also have to overcome. This is why the person who reads it often will be blessed according to The Revelation 1:3:

> "Blessed is he that readeth, and they that hear the words of this prophecy, and keep those things which are written therein: for the time is at hand."

There was only one Church which represented the believers who overcame everything Jesus warned the Churches. The only other Church not rebuked which will obviously NOT meet the LORD in the rapture was the Church of Smyrna which will die martyrs death before the rapture occurs.

I believe in the rapture. I decided a long time ago, whenever it takes place I am going! I am a pre-tribber, not because some Bible scholar taught it, but because the Spirit of the LORD revealed it to me. I saw the pre-tribulation rapture clearly in The Revelation 3. The only Church that was given the promise of the rapture was the church of Philadelphia. It was the Church of "Brotherly love" which is the meaning of the name. Look at this passage of scripture from Revelation 3:7-13:

> "And to the angel of the church in Philadelphia write; These things saith he that is holy, he that is true, he that hath the key of David, he that openeth, and no man shutteth; and shutteth, and no man openeth; I know thy works: behold, I have set before thee an open door, and no man can shut it: for thou hast a little strength, and hast kept my word, and hast not denied my name. Behold, I will make them of the synagogue of Satan, which say they are Jews, and are not, but do lie; behold, I will make them to come and worship before thy feet, and to know that I have loved thee. Because thou hast kept the word of my patience, I also will keep thee from the hour of temptation, which shall come upon all the world, to try them that dwell upon the earth. Behold, I come quickly: hold that fast which thou hast, that no man take thy crown. Him that overcometh will I make a pillar in the temple of my God, and he shall go no more out: and I will write upon him the name of my God, and the name of the city of my God, which is new Jerusalem, which cometh down out of heaven from my God: and I will write upon him my new

name. He that hath an ear, let him hear what the Spirit saith unto the churches."

I began preaching the Gospel in August 1983, and all these years I have avoided teaching eschatology because invariably it caused questions to arise regarding the rapture of the Church. I have not denied it by any means but I have never brought forth any doctrinal teaching on the subject. You may ask why. It's simple. I refuse to teach another man or woman's revelation. I certainly believe many have had the scriptures on this subject revealed to them and I welcome their teaching. It has given me much to meditate upon, but I myself had not had it revealed to me personally until November 2015.

My brief testimony about that revelation goes something like this:

I was leading a prayer service before our Sunday morning church meeting and I was praying that we would have open doors when the LORD reminded me of the above passage in Revelation. So right away after prayer I sat down alone to read it. Several things immediately stood out to me from this passage:

- The message is written to the church of "brotherly love."

- The LORD set before them an "open door" that no man can shut!

- This is the only Church who is given the "open door" promise.

- The apostate church will one day worship at their feet and recognize God's love for them.

- Because this church is patient and has not denied the LORD's Name they will be KEPT from the hour of temptation that will come upon every person on earth.

- Because this church overcomes they will be made pillars in the temple of God.

- They will never go out of the temple again.

- The temple is in the New Jerusalem that will come down out of heaven.

- They will overcome by simply holding fast to their crown (righteousness).

All these points clearly reveal this church and only this church will be removed from the earth before the rapture. They will be placed in the Temple which is in the New Jerusalem which will come down out of heaven. The promise of the crown of righteousness is strongly connected with the appearing of the LORD to His church. We see this in 2 Timothy 4:8:

> "Henceforth there is laid up for me a crown of righteousness, which the Lord, the righteous judge, shall give me at that day: and not to me only, but **unto all them also that love his appearing**."

Then just a few verses later I read these words from Revelation 4:1.

> "After this I looked, and, behold, **a door was opened in heaven**: and the first voice which I heard was as it were of a trumpet talking with me; which said, **Come up hither**, and I will shew thee things which must be **hereafter**."

Immediately after this call to go through the door in heaven, John was in the Spirit and saw the throne of God.

51

When I read "a door was opened in heaven" and realized that the timing of it was just before the beginning of the Great Tribulation I just about came unglued!

Suddenly I was filled with joy. I leaped out of my seat and ran to share it with my Pastor. He was glad that I had seen it for myself, but I don't think he had ever questioned the pre-tribulation rapture theory as I had done. So, his joy was not as exuberant as mine because the revelation did not mean as much to him as it did to me.

For the first time in my life I had a confidence there was indeed a group of believers who would be removed from the earth before the Great Tribulation. Since that time I have never doubted it. I knew I had my answer from the Word of God which was confirmed in my heart by the Spirit of God. These are believers who love God with "all" their hearts, with "all" their minds, with "all" their strength and love their brothers and sisters as they love themselves.

"All" is a shocking word when you consider that it means 100%. Not 99.9%. I believe God is redefining our idea of love. Loving Him with all our being transcends every desire of our hearts. In other words, Jesus wants ALL our desire first to be Him. That can make me shake in my spiritual boots! I don't want to pursue that thought because there is so much more I want to address, but I encourage you to let the Holy Spirit minister to you as I have about how that little-big word ALL applies to you and your desires.

Those who love God will love who God loves. I think the Father loves the body of Christ as much as He loves His Son which is more than anything else in or out of this universe. So in my line of thinking it follows that those who love God will also love the body of Christ. They will even be willing to lay down their lives for one another. In fact, I believe this describes the church of Philadelphia, the church of brotherly love. They will be patient with their brothers and sisters in Christ and will forgive those who persecute them for righteousness sake.

Through their ability to stand firm for God's love and His truth in the face of opposition, they will deliver many who are now deceived. I also believe the real persecution against true believers in America will come from those who refuse the love and truth that overcoming believers offer. Even now many are being drawn away from the true Gospel. They have itching ears. They only want to hear sweet, positive words of love and grace devoid of truth. Many of these are already demonized and controlled by deceiving and seducing spirits. Look at 2 Thessalonians 2:7-12:

> "For the mystery of iniquity doth already work: only he who now letteth will let, until he be taken out of the way. And then shall that Wicked be revealed, whom the Lord shall consume with the spirit of his mouth, and shall destroy with the brightness of his coming: Even him, whose coming is after the working of Satan with all power and signs and lying wonders, And with all deceivableness of unrighteousness in them that perish; because they received not the love of the truth, that they might be saved. And for this cause God shall send them strong delusion, that they should believe a lie: That they all might be damned who believed not the truth, but had pleasure in unrighteousness."

Okay I am about to share with you a revelation that will shock some of you. I do not believe the one restraining the antichrist take-over is the Holy Spirit! Why? Because if the Holy Spirit was removed from the earth no one could be saved during the Great Tribulation! Think about it. No one can come to the LORD unless the Holy Spirit draws him. Eschatology Scholars have been teaching this amiss for years – in my opinion. One of the chief works of the Holy Spirit is to draw sinners to Jesus, to anoint preachers to preach, to cause the LORD's people to know His voice and lead them into the knowledge of the truth. These activities of the Spirit of God will still be taking place during those terrible seven years of great tribulation.

But before the great tribulation, the overcoming Church who loves the LORD and loves His body will hold back the tide of evil through prayers, declarations and decrees by the power and authority of the Holy Spirit. When the overcoming Church is removed by the rapture then there will be no one to restrain the antichrist system from taking complete control of the entire world.

I do not believe many of us in America are ready yet. God loves us so much that He is presently dealing with us through many hard corrections. However, I believe the LORD is going to do a miracle. He is going to reveal Himself to His Church and that mighty vision will shake us out of lethargy and selfishness and desire for money and pleasures of this world.

God will make His Church in America ready. Let us cry together, "Yes LORD! Make yourself known to us very soon. Let us see your glory. We must have a fresh revelation of You!"

Then a revival such as the world has never seen will draw millions of sinners to the LORD Jesus Christ. The revival may not last long, but it will be powerful. Those of us who are ready will be very busy! By the power and authority in the Name of Jesus, we will do many miracles, signs and wonders.

CHAPTER 9

TWO MORE THOUGHTS

Number one, I believe there is another valid interpretation to this God-given night vision, and it has to do with the direction in which the LORD was traveling. He came out of the East, then turned and galloped with great speed toward the North.

In many places when the Scriptures refer to the North, God is referring to the enemies of Israel. Also, the Nation of Israel lies to the East of America. We are her allies. The LORD will reveal His glory to us, His Church, and we are one with His people Israel. He is going forth to destroy His enemies – both Israel's and ours and He will beckon us to follow. He will strengthen us to war. This is not a physical war, but a war against evil spirits that are holding the souls of men and women and children in bondage.

When the LORD reveals himself to the believers in America I believe He will simultaneously reveal Himself to the children of Israel who hunger for righteousness. What a day that will be. The believers of Israel and the Gentile believers of America will become one. Hallelujah!

Number two, in the night vision when we beheld His glory, great joy filled our little vehicle. Great joy regardless of our circumstances will come upon us at the same time as the glory. Psalm 149:5 says,

> "Let the saints be joyful in glory: let them sing aloud upon their beds."

It says, "In their beds." That is in the night time.

The psalmist said, "Let the saints be joyful in glory." Does that mean that without glory there isn't much joy? Think about that. Or maybe it means joy will be automatic in

glory. If you consider the meaning again of "doxa" –
"everything that God is and everything that God has,"
well, I think it just goes without saying that you can't help
but have joy if you have all that! And here is a little more
proof: 1 Peter 4:13:

> "But rejoice, inasmuch as ye are partakers of
> Christ's sufferings; that, when his glory shall be
> revealed, ye may be glad also with exceeding joy."

How great will our joy be when we all get a vision of His
glory - at the same time? I can't imagine.

I'm beginning to realize that glory is all over the Bible but
in the past I rarely ever saw it. It seems to be one of those
imperceptible words that only a revelation can bring out.
May the LORD reveal His glory to us and in us very soon.

CHAPTER 10

So, I'm Just Saying

Do you remember in the night vision, that The LORD, the chariot and the horses seemed to be made of transparent glass, and had the appearance of liquid, molten gold? Looking at them was like gazing into the opening of a glass-blower's furnace. Just for grins look at The Revelation chapter 21, verses 21-26:

> "...and the street of the city was pure gold, as it were transparent glass. And I saw no temple therein: for the Lord God Almighty and the Lamb are the temple of it. And the city had no need of the sun, neither of the moon, to shine in it: for the glory of God did lighten it, and the Lamb is the light thereof. And the nations of them which are saved shall walk in the light of it: and the kings of the earth do bring their glory and honour into it. And the gates of it shall not be shut at all by day: for there shall be no night there. And they shall bring the glory and honour of the nations into it."

So, make of it what you will but I'm just saying, I know I've had a tiny glimpse of His glory which seems to be the stuff of which the heavenly Jerusalem is made! This little bit of glory I witnessed in the night vision has held me spellbound for more than 24 years. I can't imagine what I'll do when it actually comes to earth.

I watch for it. I long for it. I believe it. I know it's coming. Amen.

The End

Deborah has been a Missionary/ Evangelist/ Pastor since 1983. If you want to contact her for meetings, questions or comments, feel free to reach her at:

rev.deb@hotmail.com

Printed in Great Britain
by Amazon